Published by Sterling Publishing Co., Inc.
387 Park Avenue South, New York, NY 10016

© 2006 Nina Chertoff and Susan Kahn

Distributed in Canada by Sterling Publishing
c/o Canadian Manda Group, 165 Dufferin Street,
Toronto, Ontario, Canada M6K 3H6

Distributed in the United Kingdom by GMC Distribution Services,
Castle Place, 166 High Street, Lewes, East Sussex, England BN7 1XU

Distributed in Australia by Capricorn Link (Australia) Pty. Ltd.
P.O. Box 704, Windsor, NSW 2756, Australia

ISBN-13: 978-1-4027-3896-8
ISBN-10: 1-4027-3896-X

10 9 8 7 6 5 4 3 2 1

For information about custom editions, special sales, premium and
corporate purchases, please contact Sterling Special Sales
Department at 800-805-5489 or specialsales@sterlingpub.com.

Sterling Publishing Co., Inc.
New York

CELEBRATING
Christmas
ORNAMENTS

By Nina Chertoff and   Susan Kahn

Introduction

We all have our favorite Christmas ornament. It may be a delicate glass pear tree passed down from a loving aunt, or a paper cutout of Santa made proudly in kindergarten decades ago. Whatever the shape, size, or material, ornaments are what make our Christmas trees so special.

Christmas is such an enormous holiday in the United States it may seem surprising to learn that it was not widely celebrated here until the 1800s. And even then, because of the influence of our no-nonsense Puritan ancestors, decorated trees were not common.

But gradually, the idea of adorning evergreens took hold, and trees began to be decorated with nuts and fruits, followed by paper decorations and baked goods, sometimes whimsically shaped. Popcorn and cranberries and bits of string or yarn were placed on the trees. Homemade was the operative word.

That changed in the 1840s, when Germany began producing ornaments made possible by a new glass-blowing process. Known as kugels, they were immensely popular in Europe, and Americans became acquainted with them when German immigrants arrived with their shimmering, glistening glass decorations. The ornaments came in an ever-increasing variety of shapes: hearts, stars, saints, animals, bells—charming, delicate decorations that turned an already lovely fir tree into a glittering celebration.

As decorated trees became more and more popular in the U.S., a business

exceed a dime, they were affordable to most Americans. Now beautiful German ornaments could be bought by millions of people, and the popularity of Christmas trees grew exponentially. The decorated trees were made even more beautiful by the addition of electric lights, made available in 1882 when Edward Johnson, an associate of Thomas Edison's, created strings of lights for trees.

German imports ceased during World War I; but once the war was over, they began again, along with ornaments from Japan and Czechoslovakia, which produced lovely beaded and glass designs.

World War II again stopped imports, and it was at this time that an American company, Corning Glass, developed its own ornament business. The company had perfected a machine that could manufacture glass ornaments quickly. During the war years, it produced very American and patriotic designs, coveted by collectors today. After the war, there was a resurgence of imports

opened in 1851 in the Catskill area of New York State that grew and sold nothing but Christmas trees. And in 1889 the White House displayed its first Christmas tree, beginning a ritual that continues to this day.

By the 1880s, sales for commercially produced decorations had risen dramatically because F.W. Woolworth had begun importing German glass ornaments to its stores. Woolworth's, as those of us with long memories know, was a five-and-ten-cent store; and while its prices could from Germany and Japan, as well as from Poland and Czechoslovakia.

At the same time that new materials were being developed for ornaments, their packaging was changing. In the early 1970s, Hallmark began selling ornaments in single packages. While still inexpensive, the ornaments took on a custom look, and they were very successful. By the 1980s, the market grew again when Christopher Radko began making unique blown-glass ornaments in European workshops and sold them in the U.S. in individual packages as well. From a mass commodity, ornaments now became singular things of beauty.

Today the variety of Christmas decorations available is startling, and the number of collectors is enormous. But whether you are a collector or simply an admirer, you will find on the following pages a spellbinding array of some of the most creative, clever, and beautiful ornaments ever produced.

Christmas Ornaments 1840-1960

A Merry Christmas

Ornaments in the early Victorian period were often homemade, and were textured, bright, and whimsical. Of the commercially produced decorations, the most popular were paper. By the end of the 19th century, interest in homemade ornaments lessened, and Americans began importing glass-blown ornaments from Germany, called kugels. F.W. Woolworth's was the first company to import them in large quantities, and in just a few years, the chain had sold $25 million worth. By the 1930s, 95 percent of all the ornaments on American Christmas trees came from Germany. Most were glass, but the embossed and pressed-paper ornaments made by artisans in Dresden, Germany, were also popular. Other imports included ornaments made of pressed tin. In the 1930s, the Matchless Electric Company began producing Matchless Stars, which were glass points surrounding a lighted glass center. Another new material, celluloid, was used in the 1930s and 40s but was replaced in the 1950s by plastic, a safer, more durable choice for ornaments.

Victorian

During the Victorian period, many ornaments were made by children, who cut and pasted designs on cardboard figures and added decorative material. Parents sometimes put small toys and cornucopias on trees.

A popular ornament was the paper candleholder, which, however, was highly flammable. Many early decorations were quite elaborate, as the lovely ones here illustrate.

A Merry Christmas

Boxes

Specially printed cardboard boxes full of candies were manufactured in the United States for the Christmas season. They were designed so that they could be hung on Christmas trees once the candy was eaten. Tens of thousands were made each year, and many were handed out in churches. The triangular box is the oldest of the group, dating back to 1910.

OPEN AND EXAMINE

MERRY CHRISTMAS TO YOU ALL

All of these glimmering glass ornaments are silver, except for the two at far upper right, which are painted.

On this page are two fantasy ornaments, which were free-blown designs created by the glass blower. They often had extensions that held other ornaments, and were very popular in the 1920s and '30s. At far right is a shoe from the 1930s. The clown is also from the '30s, and is Russian.

17

An appealing array of ornaments. The Santa is from the 1920s, and the unusual bird from the 1930s. The fish is probably from the 1930s as well, and the little chimney sweep is from the 1950s.

Americana

Patriotic fervor affected the look of many ornaments after World War I. These fine Uncle Sams are celluloid and were made in the 1930s. On the opposite page at upper left is an 1899 ornament that was actually a paper candleholder. The umbrella and horn are blown glass from the 1930s, and the bell is from the 1920s.

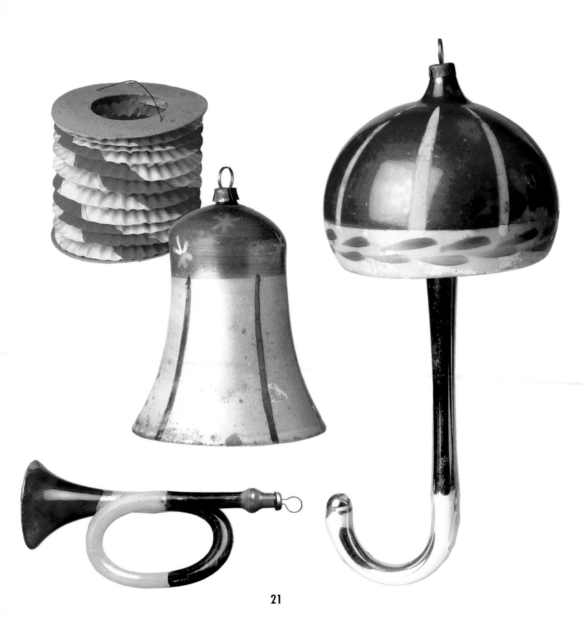

22

Americana is reflected in these charming glass-blown ornaments from the 1920s and 1930s. The bird's tail is made of spun glass.

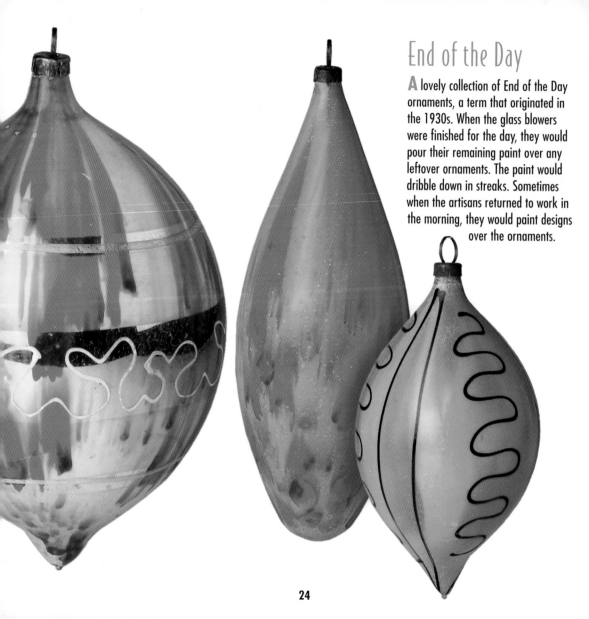

End of the Day

A lovely collection of End of the Day ornaments, a term that originated in the 1930s. When the glass blowers were finished for the day, they would pour their remaining paint over any leftover ornaments. The paint would dribble down in streaks. Sometimes when the artisans returned to work in the morning, they would paint designs over the ornaments.

26

Santas

Clearly a favorite subject for ornaments, Santa comes in all shapes and with varying expressions. These glistening blown-glass ornaments are European and from the '20s and '30s. The pinecone Santa probably appeared a little later.

Rare celluloid Santas are at far left and far right. These were made as children's toys, even though celluloid is easily broken as well as highly flammable. Understandably, few have survived. The celluloid Santas are joined by two fine glass ornaments at near left and a jolly Santa from the early 1950s. He's made of chenille and has a die-cut paper face.

Soulful Santa on the left was also a candy container. His face is made of a pre-plastic composite.
At right is a blown-glass ornament surrounded by a painted bottle brush frosted with homemade snow (probably cotton). Both are from the 1930s.

Celluloid

Celluloid, a precursor to plastic, was once used to make everything from knife handles to toys to, yes, ornaments. Its nature is highly flammable, however, and ornaments are no longer made from this material. This charming sunbather, incongruous as she might be for a Christmas tree, was made in Japan, as were the captivating celluloid figures at right.

Plastics

Celluloid gave way to sturdier, safer plastic, which became a popular material for ornaments in the 1950s. These charming plastic angels are sitting on bells dusted with mica.

These cheerful plastic figures are typical of the ornaments of the 1950s. The lamb slightly preceded the others, appearing in 1948 as part of a boxed set of eight glow-in-the-dark animals.

Companions of the glow-in-the-dark lamb on the previous page. The animals were sold in a boxed set.

Christmas Ornaments
1960-2006

By 1960, most trees displayed a potpourri of ornaments: designs in a variety of materials, shapes, and colors, all in glorious profusion. A big change in how they were designed and sold came in 1973, when Hallmark popularized individually packaged ornaments with its Keepsake line. At first, these were glass balls with painted scenes and figures meant to commemorate a particular holiday occasion, such as a baby's first Christmas. Later, the decorations became more elaborate, sometimes playing music. By the 1980s, the luxury market had entered the field, and companies such as Baccarat, Steuben, Lalique, and Swarovski had begun marketing limited numbers of very expensive, unique ornaments.

In many cases the companies create only one new design a year.

Couture designer Versace designed these opulent porcelain ornaments in 1990. They were produced by Rosenthal. They represent Medusa and Cortège de Noël.

Two gorgeous gold-plated ornaments from Fabergé.

Exquisite designs are shown at left: The Nativity scene by Baldwin and the Rosebud by Fabergé. The Pagoda above is a very rare Tiffany & Co. sterling silver ornament with a gold-plate overlay. It was produced 25 years ago. The Coronation Egg, by Fabergé, is gold plated with enamel.

Two lovely Sarabella ornaments. They are blown glass, hand-painted by the artist, and decorated with crystals and pearls. Even the ribbons are designed to match. Sold exclusively at Bergdorf Goodman in New York City, they cost over $300 each.

Elegant is the word to describe the snowflake and the star pictured here. Both are by Swarovski.

Swarovski created these resplendent snowflakes especially for Marshall Field's stores.

51

At left, a very special Swarovski crystal floral design created for Marshall Field's. At right is an ornament called Cascade, made by Swarovski in 2005. Only 200 pieces were created, to commemorate the final year of the famed original Marshall Field's department store. Each sold for $200.

Twinkling Baccarat crystal stars
were made exclusively for Neiman
Marcus. One of the stars has gold
within the crystal. The Swarovski
hearts are multifaceted.

At left is a gorgeous Waterford ornament created in 2005 as part of its Maharajah Collection. Each ornament opens to reveal an elephant or a panda. Above is a replica of the crystal ball that drops in New York City's Times Square on New Year's Eve. It is made by Waterford. In 2005, Waterford produced the lovely bell at right; each clapper is different, representing the Twelve Days of Christmas. Shown here is a turtledove.

Sarabella created these sumptuous ornaments. Both are embellished with crystals and pearls.

60

Made in Poland by Mostowski, the Sentry and the Peacock are made of blown glass and are enclosed in crystal.

Made for Neiman Marcus, these Mostowski ornaments are exquisitely designed.

Three Mostowski ornaments; all are embellished with Swarovski crystals.

More stunning examples of Mostowski's work-manship: a sailing ship and bejeweled eggs in a basket are surrounded by crystal.

Merry Christmas 1999

William Jefferson Clinton
& Family

J. Reed and Sons created the two ornaments here in honor of President Clinton. On the left is the White House, shown with the inscription that appears on its reverse side. At right is a saxophone created in 1998 for President Clinton. Only three were made.

Sterling silver ornaments are very special—and costly. The soldier was created by Tiffany & Co., the rocking horse by Halls of Kansas City, and the drummer boy is by J. Reed and Sons. The Museum of Fine Arts in Boston commissioned this magnificent angel from J. Reed and Sons.

Mickey Mouse is fully articulated and extremely rare. It was created by J. Reed and Sons for Disneyland for its first Collectibles Festival in 1999, and only 100 pieces were made.

Santa's Helper, a 1970s ornament, was made by Gorham.

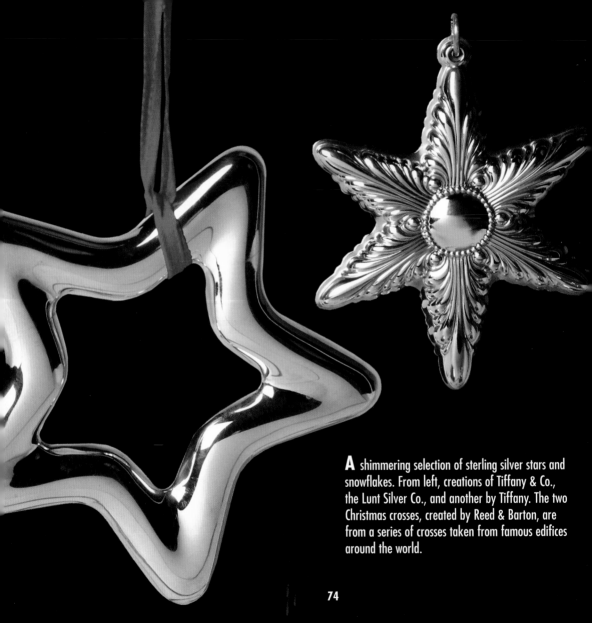

A shimmering selection of sterling silver stars and snowflakes. From left, creations of Tiffany & Co., the Lunt Silver Co., and another by Tiffany. The two Christmas crosses, created by Reed & Barton, are from a series of crosses taken from famous edifices around the world.

74

Walt Disney World was the inspiration for each of these ornaments. The Magic Castle was created by Sarabella. Only 25 were produced for the Christmas Convention in 1999. Minnie Mouse and Uncle Scrooge were created by the artist Susan Nardine Pratt.

Animal lovers will recognize the distinctive artwork of Lynn Chase in all three of these porcelain ornaments. A percentage of sales went to the Wildlife Preservation Committee.

More artistic ornaments from the talented Lynn Chase.

rtist Thomas Blackwell created these two magnificent ornaments for the Neqwa Art Co. in Texas. Elegantly designed of porcelain and painted from the inside, they were made in limited editions.

Kurt Adler of New York developed the idea for
this fun Alice in Wonderland boxed set of
blown-glass figures. They were manufactured
by the Polonaise Collection in a limited edition.

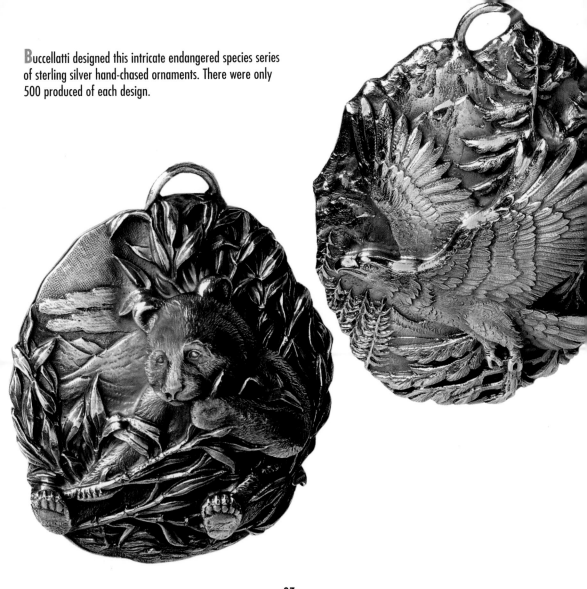

Buccellatti designed this intricate endangered species series of sterling silver hand-chased ornaments. There were only 500 produced of each design.

Swarovski crystals adorn this opulent porcelain set produced in France for Dillard's.

Whimsical designs from the Wayout Bugs Collection produced by Dept. 56 from the Krinkles Collection are done in fabulous colors. The ladybug ornament on the right was produced by Slavic Treasures and the face is that of well-known ornament collector Clara Scroggins.

Rare Christmas ornaments in which the tops open to reveal a figure inside, these very elaborate Mostowski ornaments contain a royal coach and beautiful blown-glass tree. Both were produced by Kurt Adler. The one on the right is part of the Nutcracker Suite Collection.

93

Jay Strongwater, who also produces beautiful jewelry designed the Salamander on the left. The blown-glass Tutenkommen group, at right is a limited edition from Kurt Adler.

The mummy and the barge are from the same
Tutenkommen Collection as on the previous two pages.

97

Ornaments to Remember has created tree decorations that also function as souvenirs. This kimono and little dress are of blown glass. The dress is sequined.

The purse accompanies the dress on the previous page. Santa's outfit is textured and splendidly designed.

101

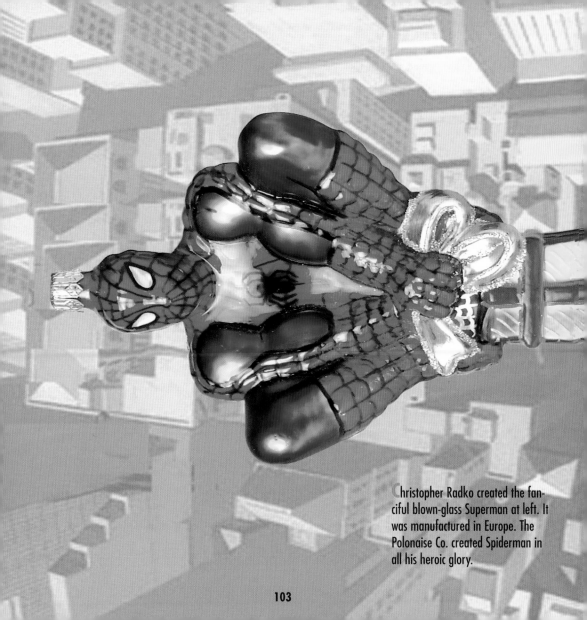

Christopher Radko created the fanciful blown-glass Superman at left. It was manufactured in Europe. The Polonaise Co. created Spiderman in all his heroic glory.

These luxurious bugs of blown glass are European.
They have the look of fine jewelry.

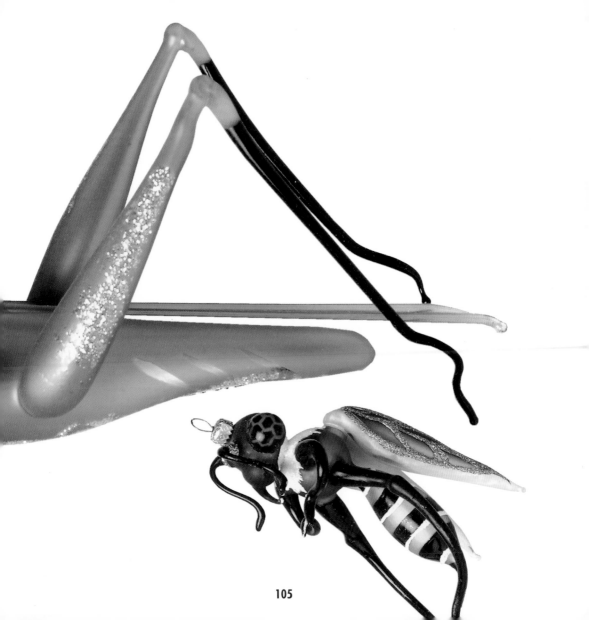

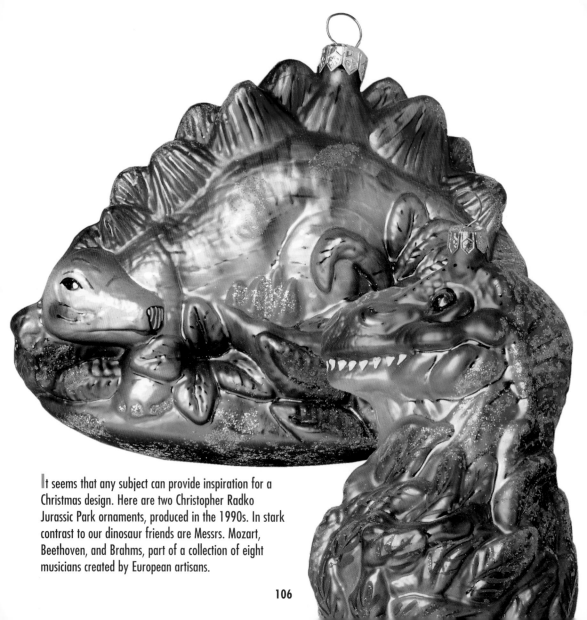

It seems that any subject can provide inspiration for a Christmas design. Here are two Christopher Radko Jurassic Park ornaments, produced in the 1990s. In stark contrast to our dinosaur friends are Messrs. Mozart, Beethoven, and Brahms, part of a collection of eight musicians created by European artisans.

These limited edition globes were sold for only one year at Gucci stores. The Fabergé Orange Tree by Whitehurst is no longer made and is highly coveted.

The wonderful blown-glass Santas at left were produced in limited numbers by Reed & Barton. Each was signed. Waterford created the enchanting traveling Santa at right, called Northern Flight.

Eckerd Drugs manufactured the two adorable hand-painted Santas below for only a short period of time. At right is a rare blown-glass ornament created by Waterford.

The Nutcracker has always been a Christmas favorite. These ornaments, all handcrafted by a Russian artist, were done by G. DeBrekht and sold as a set.

More characters from the same Nutcracker set.

And the final Nutcracker ornaments.

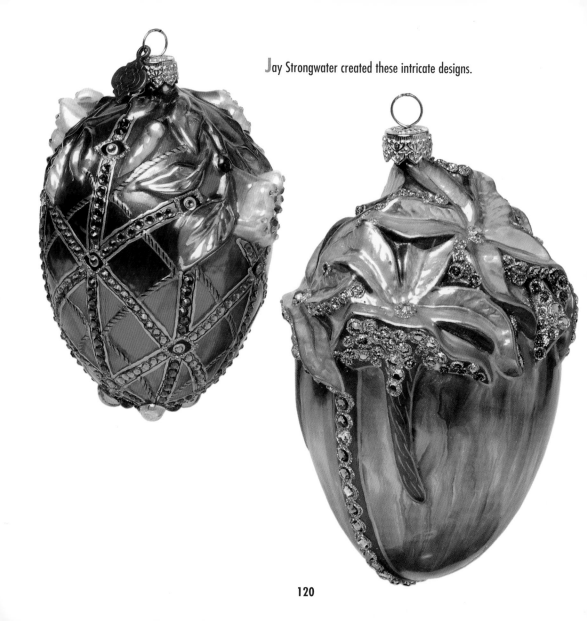

Jay Strongwater created these intricate designs.

121

Modern, simple, and stunning, these crystal ornaments were created by William Yeoward for Neiman Marcus and Bergdorf Goodman.

The Nativity scene on the left has a sterling silver overlay on fine porcelain and was created by Emelia Castillo. Only 50 were produced. The two ornaments in the center are porcelain and gold and represent two of the Twelve Days of Christmas. They are part of a set produced by Cybis Fine Art Porcelain Co. and presented to President and Mrs. Clinton. The ornament below is also by Emelia Castillo.

Lenox created the delicate ornaments at left. The cone was made in 1991 and the ball in 1982. Above is the magnificent porcelain ornament Spode designed for the millennium in 2000. Royal Doulton produced the intricately designed form at right.

The lovely ball at far left is part of the River Collection by Spode. Tiffany & Co. created the elegant balls shown at left and on this page.

Limoges of France produced these gleaming hand-painted balls in their unmistakable porcelain. They were made for Tiffany & Co. The Tiffany box is also of porcelain.

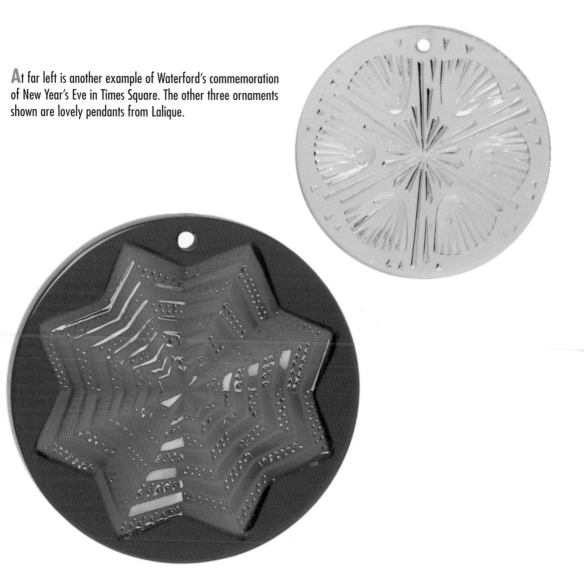

At far left is another example of Waterford's commemoration of New Year's Eve in Times Square. The other three ornaments shown are lovely pendants from Lalique.

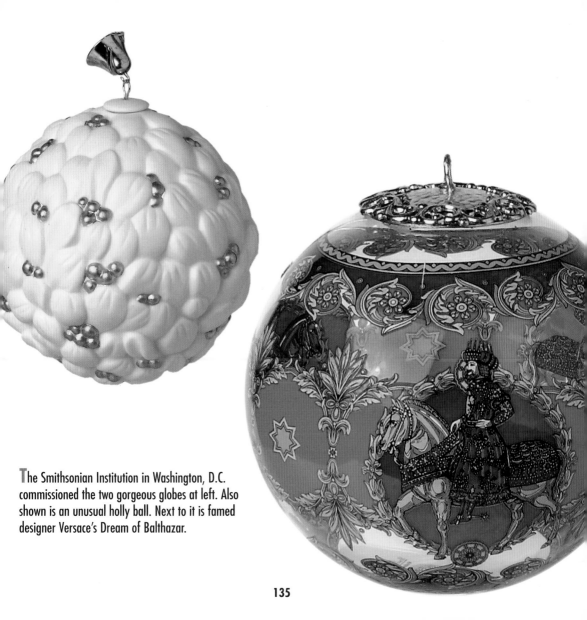

The Smithsonian Institution in Washington, D.C. commissioned the two gorgeous globes at left. Also shown is an unusual holly ball. Next to it is famed designer Versace's Dream of Balthazar.

Jay Strongwater created the lavish ornament at left and these two bejeweled tigers. The tigers are of blown glass. The smaller one is hand painted in silver and was a special edition. The larger one is embellished with Swarovski crystals.

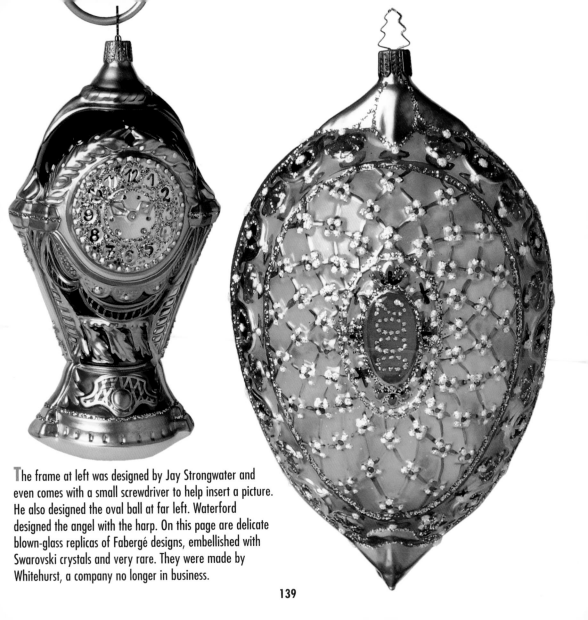

The frame at left was designed by Jay Strongwater and even comes with a small screwdriver to help insert a picture. He also designed the oval ball at far left. Waterford designed the angel with the harp. On this page are delicate blown-glass replicas of Fabergé designs, embellished with Swarovski crystals and very rare. They were made by Whitehurst, a company no longer in business.

140

Vivian Alexander created these ornaments. From left to right, Oriental Amber, *Ocean's 12,* Royal Red, Ladybug, Mardi Gras and Oriental Odyssey.

The Barbie ornament by Hallmark is hand painted and was created for collector Clara Scroggins. The disc was created by P. Buckley Moss, a well-known artist, who gave it to Ms. Scroggins. The Hallmark card shop ornament was created for the company's Keepsake members. On the window it says "Clara's."

142

This Santa was made for Eckerd Drugs and has a list of Clara Scroggins's relatives and friends. Seton McGlennon painted the ornament at right that features Clara's house.

145

Another excellent example of a custom-designed ornament, this one, created by artist Dale Mureno, commemorates the Connecticut home of a family who moved to Florida.

The lavish egg shape at left is blown glass and was produced by Whitehurst. Next to it is an exquisite design made by Jim O'Leary for Waterford. The International Silver Co. produced the sterling silver and enamel ornament at right. It represents the first of the Twelve Days of Christmas and is dazzling in its simplicity.

150

Hand painted on blown glass, the Waterford globe at left is a special edition. On this page is a beautiful cut-crystal Waterford globe that gleams like a ruby.

The large frosted blown-glass globe at left, with its dreamy images of a snowy winter scene, was created by the Mia Co. On this page are two Wedgwood pieces, both of white bisque. The cut design is especially unusual.

2000

St. Alban created the lovely sterling silver ball with a raised design, below. On the opposite page is the silver-plated sleigh bell that Wallace creates annually. The Tiffany & Co. ball in the middle is quite rare, and the Fabergé crown is absolutely royal when it opens to reveal a blue crystal.

Both of these artistic ornaments were part of the Andy Warhol Collection created by Rosenthal in 1992. They were sold only in Germany.

Celebrating Our Collectors

We are grateful to Bob and Sandy Fellows and Clara Johnson Scroggins for allowing us to photograph a small part of their astonishing collections, and for providing us with so much fascinating information.

Bob and **Sandy Fellows** have been collectors of all things Christmas for twenty-five years. When they attended their first Golden Glow of Christmas Past convention in 1991, they discovered the alluring world of vintage Christmas and began collecting, and then decorating their home with ornaments, lights, and other wonderful mementoes of Christmases long ago.

Clara Johnson Scroggins has collected Christmas ornaments for more than thirty-four years. She has over one million ornaments, the largest privately held collection in the world. Mrs. Scroggins is a meticulous historian and has written nine collectors' guides. She has been on the cover of *Franklin Mint* magazine and has been interviewed on CNN, *Good Morning America*, and HGTV. Articles about her have appeared in *The New York Times*, *USA Today*, *Southern Living*, *Home and Garden Magazine* and many other publications. She lives in Florida, with her husband Joe.

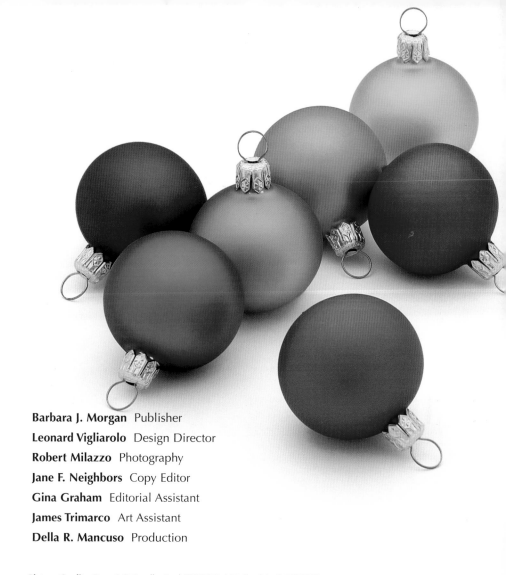

Barbara J. Morgan Publisher
Leonard Vigliarolo Design Director
Robert Milazzo Photography
Jane F. Neighbors Copy Editor
Gina Graham Editorial Assistant
James Trimarco Art Assistant
Della R. Mancuso Production